The

40 Hour Work

YEAR

The

40 Hour Work

YEAR

Become a Passive Investor

In Your Own Business!

40hourworkyear.com

Scott Fritz

This book is dedicated to my wife, Jennifer, who, for better or worse, has stuck with me and endured the life of an entrepreneur's wife for almost twenty years.

It is also dedicated to entrepreneurs around the world who wake up at 3:00 AM with an idea they can't get out of their head and use their passion and guts to get their butts out of bed and do whatever it takes to turn that idea into reality!

Author's Note

In the summer of 2007, I was asked to give a presentation to a group of entrepreneurs who belong to an incredible organization I have been a member of for almost a decade, the Entrepreneur's Organization (EO). One of the members of this group is a good friend of mine, and he wanted me to tell my story to his fellow forum members.

My story? He wanted me to explain how someone who owned a company with annual revenues in excess of 170 million dollars could live two thousand miles away from company headquarters and only "work" forty hours a year.

As an entrepreneur who is always up for a challenge, I said sure ... but then I had to figure out how I was going to put together my story for a three-hour presentation.

I had spent ten years building my business from scratch, but I had never documented exactly how I got here. Six weeks later, my three-hour presentation was complete, and I was ready to tell my story. Two years and many presentations later, I finally got around to putting my story in a book ...

So, thanks, Dan, for asking me to speak to your group. Without your invitation, I highly doubt this book would exist.

Contents

1

Was I Born with It?

I believe that a big part of my passion for entrepreneurship comes from being born into an entrepreneurial family. My grandfather started, operated, and sold his own company, as did my father. Growing up in that atmosphere was quite an experience. When I think back about conversations around the dinner table as a youngster, I recall that we focused on two things and two things only: business and politics.

Although these two topics were not exactly at the top of my mind, as I was a young boy who was more interested in sports, cars, and eventually chasing girls, they would prove to be critical in helping me identify, start, and build my business.

Some of the most successful entrepreneurs I know have a similar background to mine, and some of the most successful entrepreneurs I know do not. The conclusion I have reached is that entrepreneurial genes are in all of us, but only those who find their true passion, and then focus and act on it, are able to unlock them.

Ask yourself this question: What was the first business you started? Take a minute and think back to your childhood. When I ask entrepreneurs this question, most of them have a story that dates back to when they were five to ten years old. I have heard stories about cutting lawns, shoveling snow, babysitting, painting houses, and many others. The most interesting thing to me is that all of these stories include examples of business strategies, such as sales, marketing, operations, and leadership.

My story is no different and begins at the business savvy age of eight. I had grown fond of the Jolly Rancher candy sticks that were popping up at the local corner stores all around town. One day as I was sitting on the playground enjoying an apple-flavored stick, a friend of mine asked if I had another one. As the oldest of four boys, I had already learned the power of negotiation from my siblings, so I replied, "Sure, what are you willing to pay for it?"

My friend paused and then quickly pulled out a quarter from his pocket. I smiled and asked, "Is that all you have?" He said yes, and because he was my friend, I sold him one of the candy sticks for a quarter. At the time, those sticks were selling for a dime at the grocery store and for about eight cents each when you bought a box of fifty.

I do not recall if the gravity of the event hit me at that point, but I do recall that not long after this event, I was bringing boxes of Jolly Rancher sticks to school in my backpack.

I continued to be a one-man operation, selling my candy sticks to anyone who wanted to buy them. Then one day while on recess, a couple of kids from another class asked me if I would sell them ten sticks at a time. I was intrigued by this request and asked them why were they buying so many. They told me that they were planning to sell them in art class and in the gym. Well, it was time to expand my sales force! I started buying ten boxes a week and then turned around and sold them to my sales team for two dollars over cost-per-box. I was now grossing as much from selling the boxes as I was from the individual sticks.

All was going along great with my little venture until the government (the principal) got involved and decided to regulate me out of business. I still remember my parents telling me that I was no longer able to sell my candy at school. I also remember the sheepish grin on my father's face as he gave me the news. I knew deep down that he was proud of my entrepreneurial spirit and did not want to extinguish the flame. The good news was that there was no suspension or detention, just an agreement that I would not sell anything at school ever again.

The valuable business lessons I learned from this experience "stick" with me to this day: (1) Business is relationships. (2) People do not want to be sold; they want to buy. (3) The number one way to make a sale is to ask for the business. (4) Leverage is the key to sustainable growth. (5) Stay away from highly regulated businesses.

Of course, there were also the lessons of margin, volume discounts, pricing, and others. Take a minute and think about your first business. How many lessons from that experience are still with you today?

List them below:

Throughout this book I will reference different experiences I have had as an entrepreneur. This will help to illustrate my belief that entrepreneurial genes are inside each of us. Once this passion is realized and focused on, all the entrepreneur needs is the final ingredient to live the 40 Hour Work YEAR!

Based on this Chapter:

What did I learn about my business?

What did I learn about myself?

2

The Beginning

The majority of this book's content is based on what I learned through the development, growth, and sale of a company I cofounded in 1997.

The name of the company is Human Capital, and it continues under that name today, even though I sold it over two years ago. Human Capital is a professional employer organization (or PEO) that offers human resource and employee administration outsourcing services to companies across the United States, companies ranging in size from one to one thousand employees.

The details of the business are not important for the context of this book, but I believe there are several factors regarding its business model that are key to understanding why I chose to enter this industry space and how I leveraged those factors to create the 40 Hour Work YEAR.

I always knew I would own a business someday. As I said earlier, I grew up in an entrepreneurial environment, and I had loved the challenge of building things as far back as I can remember.

It was November 1996, and my career since graduating college consisted of a five-year stint with PepsiCo and a couple of years working for smaller private companies in a managerial capacity. I had just taken a directorship position with a company located in Michigan, and they were using a PEO for their employer administration, payroll compliance, and benefit plans. Although I was familiar with payroll companies and outsourced HR services, I had never seen or been involved with a company that combined all of these essential services in one place.

After working with this PEO for about three months and dealing with the shortcomings of their service offerings, I came to the realization that *this* was the business I would start.

You know, luck and fate are all part of life, and whether you think they play a big role or a very little role (if any), I believe that starting my own PEO was meant to be.

The HR director at the company I was working for happened to see things the same way I did when it came to the PEO the company was using at the time. She also saw the opportunity this business model could offer a couple of hard-working entrepreneurs.

More interestingly, the HR director (and my future business partner) grew up in a family full of entrepreneurs, including her mother and father. So there I was: I had found my business model, an HR expert to handle the operational side of the business, and a partner who grew up in a similar business-minded environment! Like I said, it was meant to be … and I was definitely going to *act on it*.

I mentioned before that there were several factors regarding this business model that piqued my interest and helped me realize that I could be passionate and focused about this industry. I had realized many years earlier that the business I would start would need to have as many of the following characteristics as possible for me to be a successful entrepreneur. The business would need to

1. have annuity income
2. be a service business
3. have a low barrier to entry
4. have a strong cash flow
5. be scalable to reach a nationwide base

Guess what? The PEO model (when executed correctly) hit *every one* of these out of the park:

1. It had annuity income. We were paid every time a client ran a payroll. I did not have to constantly sign new clients to cover my cash flow.
2. It was a service business. No inventory or capital intensive production facility was needed.
3. It had a low barrier to entry. No licensing or technical training was required, and there was no nine-hundred-pound gorilla.

4.   It had a strong cash flow. We were paid first (electronically, multiple times a month), and then we paid our pass-through costs and overhead.

5.   It was scalable to reach a nationwide base. Once the machine was in place, I could hire others to run it. The target market was 97 percent of all businesses in the United States (the percentage of companies with less than one hundred employees).

In January 1997, while I was still working at my current job, my partner and I began spending nights and weekends putting our business plan and loan proposal together. Fast forward eight months and many sleepless nights later, and I found myself self-employed—or unemployed, depending on your point of view.

That was it. I quit my job; I had no paycheck, no benefits, no safety net, and so on. I just took that leap off the precipice that every entrepreneur eventually takes. It was both terrifying and electrifying all at the same time!

One of the things I liked about going into this industry was the fact that we did not need a lot of cash to get started. But we still needed a loan to make it through the eight months of runway that we had given ourselves to make or break it.

Neither my business partner nor I had a ton of assets to leverage at that point in time, so we turned to the Small Business Administration (SBA) for funding. For those of you thinking of using the SBA for some or all of your start-up funding, I have one piece of advice: *do not do it!*

The Bank guaranteed us that the "easier" process of using the SBA would get us our money faster, which meant getting funding in August 1997.

We turned on the lights at the end of September 1997 and did not receive one dime of funding from the SBA until January of 1998. Looking back at this five-month span of time in my life, I recall many mornings standing in the shower staring at the wall and asking myself out loud, "What have you done," and then telling myself, "I am an idiot."

I started the company knowing very little—if anything—about selling, and after my first dozen appointments, I realized that I knew even less than I thought.

I purchased at least ten sales books those first few months and started trying all of the different closing techniques on my unassuming prospects. But just as I had learned from my candy business back in grade school, people don't really want to be sold to, they want to buy.

I recalled the four Ps of success that I learned back when I was a teenager: passion, positivity, persistence, and patience. I never had a problem with the first three, but that last one was not one of my strong suits.

The year was quickly coming to an end, and I had yet to sign one client. I braced myself for the harsh reality of starting the new year with no top-line revenue, and then like flipping on a light switch, the fourth P went into payout mode.

I signed half a dozen small clients in less than two weeks and signed a very big client right before the end of the year.

At about the same time (here comes the patience again), the bank finally funded our loan, and from that point forward, we were on what can best be described as a rocket ride.

Based on this Chapter:

What did I learn about my business?

What did I learn about myself?

3

Mindset Philosophy

Now that I have given you some background regarding my upbringing and business start-up experience, I will take you through the first breakthrough I had as a business owner. I call this breakthrough my mindset philosophy.

My mindset philosophy is the guideline of how I define my life and decision-making process as an entrepreneur. I am a big believer in the power of threes, so for me, the only way to keep my mindset philosophy clear and meaningful was to create a three-tier filter.

I call this filter, my focus filter, which is comprised of the following three statements: enjoy life, make money, and do deals. For me, this is as simple and as focused as it gets. My ultimate goal for the time I am blessed to be on this planet is to enjoy life. Enjoying Life is comprised of many things, including the people I will work with, the location of the opportunity, the time involved, and the amount of hassle I may encounter. If I am seriously looking at any kind of business opportunity, it needs to provide enough revenue to make it worth doing, thus, making money. And finally, if the first two requirements are met, doing deals is next in line. Doing deals does not mean that I do every deal that passes the first two stages of my filter; it means that I move to that stage of review.

Although these statements have remained the same for over ten years, they have switched positions as my business grew and I matured.

On the following page is my current mindset philosophy as seen through my focus filter. The order of the statements has not changed since 2004.

My Mindset Philosophy Today

Enjoy Life

Transition from working in and on my business to the role of passive investor and advisory board member.

Make Money

Position my company to run as a self-sufficient profit machine, capable of growing through utilizing its own systems and executive management team.

Do Deals

Acquisition-focused company ready to begin acquiring other businesses and positioned to create an investor exit for maximum returns.

You will notice that under each tier, there is a descriptive business action word and an accompanying sentence that specifically details how I achieve each filter level.

It was critical for my success that I attached a business action word with specific details to each filter. Without these components as part of my filter, it would have been very difficult (if not impossible) to achieve the 40 Hour Work YEAR.

Once I had developed my mindset philosophy, I was ready to begin the journey to the ultimate place of enjoyment, freedom, and completeness that very few entrepreneurs ever achieve.

I would like to lead you through an exercise on the following page that will help you develop your mindset philosophy. By having you answer several key questions, you will be able to set a baseline for success and measure your progress.

EXERCISE

Take some time to answer each of these questions in the space provided below.

1. How many hours do I currently "work" every week? (For the purposes of this discussion, we will define "work" as the time you are spending working *in* and *on* your business.)

2. How many hours am I at the office each week? (These are counted within your total hours in question one, but need to be broken out for future discussion.)

3. What *one* word would my best employee or best friend use to describe me? (If you do not know, *go ask!* This is a critical data point that will accelerate the pace in which you achieve the 40 Hour Work YEAR. Remember, this must be *one* word.

1. _____

2. _____

3. _____

EXERCISE

Using the answers to the questions on the previous page, create your current Mindset Philosophy below.

My Mindset Philosophy

On the following page there is an outline of how my mindset philosophy changed over the years (by answering the three questions). Use this to see what the chronology of my philosophy looks like for purposes of developing you own.

1997–2000

Mom & Pop business / *In* the Business / Doing It

Do Deals, Make Money, Enjoy Life

Ninety-plus hours a week / Fifty-plus hours a week / Focused

2000–2004

Small Business / *On* the Business / Coaching Others to Do It

Make Money, Do Deals, Enjoy Life

Forty hours a week / Fifty hours a year / Leader

2004–2007

Enterprise Business / Passive Investor / Letting Others Do It

Enjoy Life, Make Money, Do Deals

One and a half hours a month / twenty-two hours a year / Visionary

The 40 Hour Work YEAR!

To me, the basic definition of a business owner is someone who can afford to hire an employee to do their job. Until you can afford to hire this person you don't own a business, you own a job! From 1997 to 2000, I was not taking a paycheck; I was the *only* sales person for the company. My title was CEO, and I was doing all the work myself!

Whenever I think back to this time period, I have visions of the Dunkin' Donuts commercials of my youth. In the commercial, the Dunkin' Donuts owner walked around the donut shop at four in the morning like a zombie, mumbling, "Time to make the donuts." I know that's how I felt during this bootstrap, start-up, knock-on-wood, cross-your-fingers phase of my entrepreneurial experience!

I definitely had what I call a mom-and-pop business. My focus philosophy was, in order, to do deals, make money, and maybe have a few minutes a month to enjoy life. I was all about doing deals. I wasn't focused enough on if we made any money, and I definitely wasn't enjoying life, meaning I didn't have much freedom.

I was making the donuts every day and hoping that at the end of each day, I could make it through to the next one. I was working over ninety hours a week. I was spending over fifty hours a week at the office, and my best employee, who was still with me when I sold the company, described me as focused.

So, I spent ninety-plus hours a week working, fifty-plus hours a week in the office, and I was focused. But, you realize, I was still physically at the office for over fifty hours every week. That was terrible. The last place I should have been when I was in charge of hunting down our next client was at the office.

But guess what? I wasn't just selling. I was wearing all the hats. It's the "Got a minute? Got a minute?" syndrome. I would be sitting in my office trying to complete a task or make that closing sale, and here comes that knock on the door with the phrase that strikes fear in real entrepreneurs: "Got a minute?"

I realized after I had suffered through this syndrome for several months that I must eliminate it immediately. I had to do whatever I had to do to make it go away!

My solution? I created strict rules on when people could talk to me, and I clarified that the problem better be important—not just urgent. I required that before they started knocking, they need to have thought through at least three solutions to the problem.

This system worked great and allowed me to begin developing not just managers, but leaders within the company. Before long, the knocks were coming only once a day, then once a week, and soon once a month, if at all.

Near the end of 1999, I began to realize that working *in* your business was not the way to really grow a scalable company. I needed to begin thinking bigger and looking at my business as a tool for personal growth and for creating wealth.

I started to understand that I needed to change my mindset and focus philosophy on multiple levels. I needed to stop doing and start coaching. I needed to find great people, give them the tools to succeed, and get the hell out of the way. There was just one problem with hiring a team that could accelerate the business: I couldn't afford it.

Based on this Chapter:

What did I learn about my business?

What did I learn about myself?

4

My Mirror Moment

The big selling season for the PEO industry is the fourth quarter of each year. This is due to the fact that payroll taxes reset on January 1 of each year and most benefit plans have renewal dates around the same time as well.

As 1999 drew to a close, I was having an incredible selling season, and we were poised to start 2000 with record growth and revenues. I still was not taking any money out of the company at this time. I was the only sales person, and I was putting in a minimum of a hundred hours a week making sales calls, preparing proposals, and attending enrollments. Oh yeah, I was also still CEO and dealing with all the other things that go on in a start-up operation.

It was the first week of December, and I had an incredible amount of closing proposals scheduled (eighteen to be exact). In my world, eighteen closing proposals are what a very good sales person would deliver in six weeks, and I was doing it in one. I was pumped!

I had spent about twenty hours preparing all of my proposals the weekend before this record-setting week. Ten were scheduled the first two days of the week, with the remaining eight scheduled the last three days. By Thursday around noon, I had rolled through fifteen presentations and had closed ten of those deals. I was running on fumes, adrenalin, and caffeine, and I was mentally and physically exhausted.

As I parked my car in front of a local fast food joint to grab some lunch, I started to feel a little light-headed and shaky. I looked in the rearview mirror, and I was pasty white with sweat starting to appear on my forehead. This was December in Michigan. I should not have been sweating. As I sat there wondering what was happening, my hands started to shake, and I felt like I was about to throw up, pass out, or both. I rolled down the windows, put my seat back as far as it would go, closed my eyes, and just laid there for what seemed like an hour (it was actually about twenty minutes).

I finally started to feel okay, and some color was coming back to my face. Convinced it was something I ate the day before, I went into the restaurant, ate my lunch, and headed off to my next appointment. I was too young, dumb, and broke to go see a doctor. In reality and retrospect, I probably had some sort of mini nervous breakdown.

To this day, I am not really sure what happened to me during what I now call my "mirror moment," and I have never had a similar experience since, but I made a promise to myself as I drove home that night. I told myself that I would hire at least one sales person in the next month and I would reduce the hours I worked in the business to fifty or less by the end of March 2000.

I think every entrepreneur has at least one "mirror moment" in their lives, maybe physical, maybe mental, maybe both. I know in my case, it changed my view of my business and my role in it forever.

I met my goal of hiring my first sales person two weeks later, and I hired two more sales people by the end of March. Revenues grew by over ten million dollars in the first quarter of that year, and I finally got paid! I also stopped working weekends, and I was averaging right around fifty hours a week by the end of May.

I had started to see the bigger picture and learned how to add the final ingredient to realize the 40 Hour Work YEAR—team. As true as it was in the growth and development of my company as it is today in my Angel Investing, there are three main ingredients that drive all entrepreneurial success: passion, focus, and team.

Most entrepreneurs start a business because they have a deep-seated passion. A few of them muster up enough focus to keep the venture going for one to five years, and a select few finally realize that they need a team to actually build and develop their company into an asset.

In my experience, both in the coaching and investing world, the following holds true:

About 80 percent of the entrepreneurs I meet have the passion. These people might be dreamers with an idea they love to talk about but not much else. They could be visionaries who have figured out what this passion will become if only they had some money or business education to pull it together. And then there are a few that realize passion is key, but without focus, their dream or vision will never become reality.

The group that understands they need focus equals roughly 20 percent of the entrepreneurs I have met over the last fifteen years. They have passed the dreaming and vision stage, but they usually have trouble making payroll and have yet to make any substantial personal income.

Finally, only 5 percent of the entrepreneurs I have ever met have all three components. They are a rare breed, and if I was to sit in a room with one hundred randomly selected entrepreneurs, there would be just five that could check all three boxes.

I had finally learned my lesson about the team part, checked all three boxes, and was never going back!

EXERCISE

In the space provided below, answer the following questions:

1. *Am I passionate about my business?*

If yes, what am I most passionate about?

If no, what would I rather be doing?

2. *Am I focused on my business and its key advantages?*

If yes, what are the key advantages?

If no, what areas should I focus on?

EXERCISE *(Continued)*

3.   *Do I have a team of leaders in my company?*

If yes, are they the right people to grow my business?

If no, what specific leadership areas are missing in my company?

EXERCISE

In the space provided below, rank your company as a whole from 1 to 10 on passion, focus, and team, with 10 being the highest rating. After you rank your company, write a sentence or two below each ranking explaining how you arrived at that score.

EXERCISE

In the space below, write the number ranking your company will attain on passion, focus, and team in the next six months and write a sentence or two outlining how you will make that happen.

Repeat this exercise every six months until you are at a nine or ten in each of the three key measurements. To achieve complete alignment, have your partners and key employees complete this exercise as well.

Based on this Chapter:

What did I learn about my business?

What did I learn about myself?

5

Ownership Paradox

I am going to share with you one of the biggest challenges faced by entrepreneurs: admitting that the more they are involved *in* the business, the *less* it is worth. I call this the ownership paradox

Unfortunately, most small business owners never come to this realization and ultimately end up owning a job and worse still, all of the risk. Why anyone would choose to own a job and the risk when they can go work for a company with no risk is beyond me.

As you work through the following exercises, you need to be completely honest with yourself. Do not get discouraged; realizing where you need help is the first step to a major breakthrough.

EXERCISE

1. *In the space below, draw an X*

2. *On the* **top right** *end of the X, write* "Company Value"

3. *At the* **bottom right** *end of the X, write* "Owner *IN* the Business"

With the very **top left** point of the "owner *IN* the business" line equaling you working everyday *in* the business and the furthest **bottom right** point of the "owner *IN* the business" line equaling you not working *in* the business *at all*, draw a circle of where you are currently on this line. *Be honest.*

From that circle, draw a dotted line up or down that intersects the "Company Value" line, and then draw a circle at that point.

Now you have just created a simple valuation for your company! If you want to increase the value of your company, you *must* stop working *in* your business!

Example Below:

Ownership Paradox

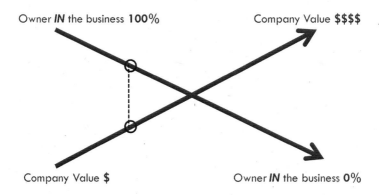

Like it or not, the company value is directly connected to how involved the owner is in the business. The point is, if entrepreneurs built companies that were system-dependent and not owner-dependent from the very beginning, the valuation would grow higher, quicker!

While conducting my coaching seminars for entrepreneurs, I am often asked if there is anything I would go back and change. As anyone who has owned a business will tell you, there are many things. But I always tell people that if I would have understood the ownership paradox from the beginning, I would have made more money much quicker.

I like to use the following example when making this point to fellow entrepreneurs. I find a house I would like to buy, and I go to the owner of the house and say, "I would like to buy your house."

They say, "Great. For one million dollars, you can buy the house, but I want to stay in it for two years after you buy it." Do I still want to buy the house?

That is the same analogy of trying to assign a value to a business where the owner will not or cannot leave.

If the only buyers I can attract need me there to make maximum returns, manage the employees, or keep the clients happy, how many buyers will there be?

The main reason it was easy to find multiple buyers and demand maximum returns when we sold our company was that my partner and I did not plan to live in our house after we sold it! We had moved out three years earlier.

From 1997 through the end of 1999, I could not move past the intersection point of the ownership paradox. I was stuck right at the cross roads of that X, and I realized I had only two choices: do nothing or make a change.

I am a big believer in the concept that the only constant is change, and I will let you in on a little secret: if I had done nothing, the danger of me staying in the business would have created limiting beliefs for myself and the company. But when I decided to make the necessary change, that same danger became a series of limitless opportunities.

EXERCISE

Where do you want to be in your life? What does that look like?

Why am I at this spot on the ownership paradox chart?

Which direction am I currently going on this chart?

What are three things I will do in the next sixty days to move further up the value line in my company?

1.

2.

3.

Based on this Chapter:

What did I learn about my business?

What did I learn about myself?

6

The Big Question

It was early April, 2001. We were living in Michigan, and it was snowing. My wife came down to the basement where I was doing some late-night work, and she said to me, "You know, you said we weren't going to live here for more than five or six years." We weren't from Michigan. We had moved there six years earlier so I could take a job opening I had been offered. She continued, "Could we move somewhere sunny and warm?"

I said, "Yeah, sure."

"Well, like in the next year?"

"Oh, okay," I said.

I spent that weekend thinking through what I really wanted to do, what my company's potential was, and how this could all come together in making my wife happy by moving somewhere sunny and warm. It became very clear to me during those couple of days that we had a huge opportunity to grow the business and that my true passion and focus was building a team and leveraging their talents to accelerate the growth curve of my company. I was not yet clear on how I would make this all work, but I knew the timing was right and it was time to take action.

This was 2001. I'm running a fifty-million-dollar company, and I was CEO. First things first, I needed to talk with my business partner and break the news to her. I met with her at a local coffee shop. I remember it vividly; I sat down and said, "We need to talk about something. I'm moving, I think to Vegas. I'm not sure, but I'm going somewhere sunny and warm."

My partner and I had a good business relationship, and although she was a little shocked, we had already discussed the fact that I was not planning on living in Michigan forever. After a brief silence, I said, "The way I see it, we have two options. You can buy me out, or we can start to develop a plan that allows both of us the freedom to not work in or on the business at all."

She said, "What exactly do you mean by 'not work at all?'"

I asked her the following question: "How much of a pay cut would you be willing to take if we could set up the company to run without us completely?"

She said, "I don't know. How much would you take?"

"I thought you would say that, so go home and talk to your husband tonight. Come up with your number, write it down on a piece of paper, and we will meet here tomorrow morning at 8:00 AM. I'll slide you my piece of paper, you slide me yours, and we'll see if we're close."

Although I am a very positive person (as are most entrepreneurs), I did not sleep very well that night. I knew that my partner did not really want to buy me out, but if we could not both agree on a number that was fair and reasonable for both of us, it could get ugly.

We met the next morning as planned, handed each other our piece of paper, and guess what happened. Unbelievably, we both had the exact same number. In my view, this was the best place we could have been because we had just eliminated a lot of the crap that could have happened if we had been way off on our numbers.

This is why I call this pivotal moment in our company's history the "big question." It was another major shift in my mindset and probably the biggest reason I was able to develop the 40 Hour Work YEAR.

I did not have the plan figured out yet; I was not even sure what the plan would be or if it would work. But just like my mirror moment, I knew that if I did not change my mindset about the business, I could not enjoy life in Las Vegas and I would be missing out on the huge opportunities that lay ahead.

So we did it. We both reduced our monthly distributions by the number we agreed to, and we put the money back into the business.

Of course, to execute the big question, we had to create a plan. If I went into my company and said, "Okay, I'm going to take a hundred-thousand-dollar pay cut. I'm going to hire someone to do my job, and then I'm moving to Las Vegas," I would never have realized the 40 Hour Work YEAR and I would not have written this book.

What we did was create a basic outline and timeline for implementation and had conversations with the three key people in our company at the time. We developed a comprehensive plan to hire people to do what we were doing, to build an executive team to eventually run the entire company, and to build systems to grow and standardize the operations of the business. I had agreed to stay in Michigan for a year to help put the basic pieces of the plan in place, with an absolute move-out date of May 2002.

I called this ultimate vision of entrepreneurial freedom the "transition plan." The name is important because the main goal and measurement of success was for the two owners to transition out of the business. It was not the strategic plan, the sales plan, the operations plan. It was the transition plan. I say this because once I decided to ask the big question and start my journey towards the 40 Hour Work YEAR, I needed to be clear about what I called the plan and the message it sent to my employees, company leaders, and future hires.

EXERCISE

Have I asked myself the big question?

If not, how large of a pay cut would I be willing to take?

What three job duties do I need to relinquish in the next six months?

1.

2.

3.

How much money would I have to spend on a monthly basis to hire someone to take over these duties?

Based on that figure, which duties will I hire someone to perform in the next six months?

Based on this Chapter:

What did I learn about my business?

What did I learn about myself?

7

Weed Eating

It was now the end of May 2001, and we had put together the basic outline and timeline of the aptly named transition plan. We briefed our key managers about the plan and the financial commitment of the owners to see the plan through to completion. I was pleasantly surprised that all of our key managers and employees were just as enthused about the journey as we were. I realized at that point that they knew the company needed to change if we were going to meet our goal of reaching a hundred million dollars in annual sales.

During this period, I really started to work on coaching others to do my work and made a conscious effort to let my employees fail from time to time so that they could learn and develop their true talents.

This is also the beginning of what I call our small business phase and the first shift in my focus philosophy. It was now ordered as: make money, do deals, enjoy life. Enjoying life still wasn't first, but I realized that any deal that would not produce the minimum margin (what we had set as a metric) was not worth doing. I would like to repeat that statement because I believe it is one of the biggest cancers in small business: *any deal that does not produce the minimum acceptable margin is not worth doing.*

This was a rather easy concept to implement when looking at new prospects, but what about those low-margin clients who were with us in the "do deals" phase and were now in their fourth year with us? I had no choice; we had to get them up to our minimum margin or let them go.

The only way we could continue to implement the transition plan without taking further pay cuts as owners was to bring on high-margin, high-quality clients and remove the low–margin clients.

I called this process "weed eating" (named after the Weedeater I used in my backyard as a kid). It was a rather simple process: we started with the clients in the lowest 5 percent margin that we had on the books at the time and raised their rates up to match those of the next lowest 5 percent's.

We completed this gradual increase over a three-month period, and the only clients that we lost were the ones who were price shoppers to begin with. We then repeated the process with the next bottom 5 percent.

By the end of 2001, we had raised up our margins by 30 percent and had only lost 2 percent of our overall client base. Guess what? All of the new businesses we added exceeded our minimum margin standards and bought our services based on value and benefits, not price and product.

We were the beneficiary of another interesting phenomenon; these top-tier clients were referring us other top-tier clients. I had removed almost all of the bottom feeders from our client pool!

I bring the weed eating concept up at this point because if we had not put our transition plan in place during this time, we would not have been forced to focus on our margins more closely or have to make some tough decisions about these clients. In addition, it enabled me to reshuffle my focus filter and to start working more *on* the business and less *in* the business.

EXERCISE

Compile your current client list and filter them through the following metrics:

1. Rank each client highest to lowest by their GROSS MARGIN on one page

2. Rank each client highest to lowest by their GROSS SALES on one page

3. Rank each client highest to lowest by their HASSLE FACTOR on one page – this is mostly subjective, but I definitely knew who my biggest hassle clients were, and if I didn't, my staff did

4. Looking at the first list, take the bottom 5% of GROSS MARGIN and highlight them

5. Now compare the highlighted list to your HIGHEST 20% in GROSS SALES list

6. Replace any client that falls within the top 20% in GROSS SALES with the next lowest client in your bottom 5% GROSS MARGIN until all of the clients that are in the bottom 5% do not appear in your top 20% in GROSS SALES list

7. Match this list with the HASSLE FACTOR ranking list and write their respective HASSLE FACTOR ranking number next to each client in your highlighted bottom 5% list

8. Adjust each of the clients margin in the bottom 5% upward to match the margin of the next lowest client (the client at the 95% ranking)

9. Starting with the client receiving the highest HASSLE FACTOR ranking and continuing through the list, Increase the client's margin % additionally as needed to reflect the amount of extra work and pain they are causing you and your staff – again, this is

mostly subjective but the idea here is to force your bottom feeder clients to leave, or get paid incredibly well for putting up with their crap!

10. Repeat the same process above every 90 days or as needed based on client acquisition

Based on this Chapter:

What did I learn about my business?

What did I learn about myself?

8

Eighty Percent

The key to implementing our transition plan was having the right people. I knew that for me to step aside and move two thousand miles away, we had to have a key leader. This was by far the most difficult position we had to fill in our company. We were fortunate enough that the individual (Seth), who ended up being the CEO and key leader of our company, was the second person we hired back in 1997. There is no magic wand or secret code for this one. In my experience, Seth worked out great for us because instead of finding a person based on a *skill set*, we promoted a leader with the right *mindset*.

I will always hire people based on mindset over skill set; it is much easier to train a person on systems and procedures than to change their behaviors and beliefs.

I need to make an important point about the attitude I had developed towards my business at this time. I am a control freak, like most everyone who is reading this book. I believe it is almost impossible to take a business through the start-up phase without having at least some tendencies of a control freak in your personality. But when it came to implementing the plan that would allow me to step away from running my business, I had to learn to let that go. To achieve this, I once again changed my mindset.

I had decided by this point that I was not going to find an exact clone of myself to take over my day-to-day job responsibilities. I also knew that whoever did replace me in the sales and marketing area would never have the passion or sense of ownership that I did. So, I resolved myself to find someone who had at least 70 percent of those qualities, and then I put a plan in place to develop another 10 percent. That's right: I was perfectly happy with replacing myself with someone who would perform at 80 percent of my abilities. Just like most of you, I have read the books and been to the seminars that preach hiring people better than you, etc.

I am not saying that hiring someone with specific skill sets (say, accounting) that are better than yours is a bad idea. I am talking about finding someone to replace me (as one of the owners) at that moment in time based on budget considerations and what we needed to accomplish over the next two years.

Once I came to terms with the idea that 80 percent of my current performance was acceptable for my replacement, I was ready to start the search and make the hire.

We also looked at the company from that same viewpoint in overall terms. If we could hire people and put a team together that would run and grow the company at 80 percent or better and not have us work *at all*, that was perfectly fine with us.

If my partner and I had not reached the 80 percent epiphany and agreed to let go of the day-to-day, the plan would *never* have worked.

Based on this Chapter:

What did I learn about my business?

What did I learn about myself?

9

The Transition

Now that I have outlined the basic ideas and principles that placed me and my company on a path to go after the 40 Hour Work YEAR, the next step is to detail the specific process that I used to transition out of my business.

The journey, as I like to call it, consisted of eight areas that we developed over roughly eighteen months. That's not to say it was a "set it and forget it" program at the end of eighteen months.

In addition, the transition plan was implemented in stages, which did not necessarily follow each other. Due to events that occurred beyond our control, as well as the business challenges we faced, portions of each of the eight areas were implemented on an as-needed, what-works-*now* basis.

We were constantly tweaking and adjusting from 2001 (when we started the program) through 2007, when we sold the company. However, what we absolutely developed over the first eighteen months was the foundation, culture, and vision for where we were going.

The eight areas that made up our transition plan, which I will go on to explain in detail, are:

1. Standard Operating Procedures—SOPs
2. Decision Matrix
3. Decision Filter
4. People Plan
5. Forecasting
6. Letting Go
7. Tracking Metrics
8. Owner Wealth & Company Value

Standard Operating Procedures

The most difficult, time-consuming, and onerous part of creating the 40 Hour Work YEAR for me was the development of the SOPs—the standard operating procedures.

I realized from my previous experiences working for large companies and franchise systems that the reason the small businesses that made up the large franchise operation were more successful than the average small business was that they had SOPs for everything.

We developed our SOPs by department and position, not by individual. Later on, when I would work with companies, they would tell me, "Oh, we've got SOPs. You know, Johnny's doing this and Mary's doing that, and Sam's doing this and Mike's doing that, and Nick's doing ..."

And I would say, "Wait a minute, so if Sam leaves or Mike goes on vacation or Mary goes on maternity leave, then what?"

SOPs must be developed by department and position. As our company grew (and so did our organization chart), setting up the SOPs by department and position made changes and alignment throughout the company very easy.

So it was the summer of 2001, and we had embarked on the six-month chore of developing the core SOPs for our company. We were moving right along, keeping to our schedule, and then the most tragic event in my lifetime occurred: 9/11.

I would like to say this was only a speed bump in our SOP development, but in reality it was a brick wall. 2002 was the only year out of ten that we did not grow by 50 percent or more, and it affected everything.

Although SOP development continued, it was at a *much* slower pace as we scrambled to keep our margins and sales flat during the downturn.

I still moved to Vegas in May of 2002, but we were forced to make some adjustments to our timetable for SOP development and implementation.

By June of 2002, we were ready for some tweaking and refining, and then we spent about three months on implementing and training, which took us right up to the peak selling season in September of 2002.

For ease of reference, I have broken down the basic process we used to develop our SOPs into the following nine steps.

1. Our first step to developing our company SOPs was to have each employee record (via a daily log book) every activity he or she engaged in each hour of the day. Every employee did this for two weeks and then turned them into their respective department managers. The rational for two weeks of recording was that we were in the payroll business, and by capturing a full two weeks of activities, we were able to cover 98 percent of our client base. For reference, we had a total of twenty-five employees completing these log books.

2. The department managers then took these logs and identified similarities between each employee's entries, ultimately refining that list into a master time log by hour and by day of the week for each department.

3. The next week we gave the master time log back to each employee and had them refine that activity list down to fifteen-minute increments for an additional two weeks. I am a big believer in the concept of "inspect what you expect," and this exercise made it very clear to the employees that we were inspecting everything.

4. The department managers again identified the similarities and developed a fifteen-minute activity log for each day of the week.

5. This step was critical. Me, my partner, and the future CEO met with each manager and had them identify the top performer in

their respective departments. We then had them compare the top performer's time log with the master list they had created and made sure we were in agreement across the board.

6. We tweaked the master log to reflect the best use of each part of the day across the entire department and started to identify key systems and procedures that would maximize every employee's productivity for each quarter-hour increment.

7. We made a list of the different systems and technologies we currently had that could be applied in a more productive manner and a list of the systems and technologies we were lacking at that time.

8. We put together a half-day meeting with all of the employees from each department to brainstorm the best practices they had been using for each part of the day and cross-referenced those with what we were currently doing in the company. Quite a few different methods were being used to achieve the same result. It became very apparent which methods (systems) were more productive. We also asked the employees what systems and technologies they thought would assist them the most in maximizing each part of the day. A lot of our employees had worked for other companies that had used different technologies than we currently had, and their input was very valuable.

9. The department manager then scheduled several meetings over the next three months with the owners and current COO (and future CEO) to develop SOPs that were in alignment with our core values and were ARMD—actionable, realistic, measurable, and dated. Using these values as a filter and making sure each SOP was ARMD made this part of the process flow smoothly and kept each department in alignment with other departments and the company. The department manager would come to

each meeting with the specific set of SOPs they were developing. The role of the owners and the COO was to evaluate, recommend, and refine each SOP until the final system for each department was 100 percent complete.

Once the SOPs were completed for each department, we documented them electronically on our company-wide intranet and paired them with the necessary forms, templates, and tracking metrics. After everything was loaded and in place, we started the next phase of SOP integration: training.

As I learned a long time ago, knowledge is not power; the application of knowledge is power. Having all of these SOPs documented and accessible on the intranet was quite an accomplishment. But if we were not going to implement them throughout the organization with a standardized, consistent training program, what was the point?

To make sure we implemented the SOP system correctly, we began with the employee hiring process. This process had its own set of SOPs that were in alignment with the on-boarding and probationary employment period. Each phase of the hiring process (search, screening, and selection) included SOPs that would ensure that when we hired a new employee, they would be a strong fit for the SOP culture we had developed.

A major component of insuring that our systems were being utilized correctly was the practice of tying the SOP performance to not only the hiring process, but to reviews and annual pay increases also. This practice was in place at every level of the company, from the CEO to the part-time mail clerk.

When each employee is hired, trained, and reviewed based on a set system of SOPs, you get alignment, you get accountability, and you get results! In my experience, this is where most small businesses fall short. They create SOPs and they do an adequate job of training and basic implementation, but they do not close the loop in the form of feedback via performance reviews and evaluations. Again, inspect what you expect.

Once our SOPs were in place and being utilized by each department, we continued to monitor them for areas of weakness and improvement. The concept of action, monitor, and modify is a simple rhythm I used with my management teams to keep continual improvement in place.

The process of ongoing review of the SOPs was done twice a year, not more than that. We did not want to get the people we were focused on training to become confused with frequent changes or inconsistencies. We gave them the tools and let them use the system we created to do the work.

Lastly, we messaged and bragged about our SOPs to our clients, vendors, and prospects. We signed some really nice accounts and showed them our SOPs as they related to each area of service they would receive.

Talk about building confidence with your customers! My competitors were ADP, Administaff, PayChex, and other big, publicly traded companies.

My clients were wiring millions of dollars a week into our bank accounts, trusting our company to pay the benefits, pay the taxes, and cut them their paychecks. If they didn't see that I have SOPs, how confident would they be in working with me?

Key points to creating SOPs

Completed by department and position

Involved every employee in the process

Is ARMD—actionable, realistic, measurable, and dated

Started at the hiring process—search, screening, and selection

Tied to reviews and evaluations for feedback and alignment throughout the company

Evaluated twice a year using the action, monitor, and modify rhythm

Messaged SOPs to clients, vendors, and prospects

Decision Matrix

As I continued along my journey in creating the 40 Hour Work YEAR, I discovered that the easiest way to remove myself from the day-to-day was to create a simple accountability system. We called this system our decision matrix.

We started by creating a list of key decisions for the company. To accomplish this quickly and to ensure alignment, we gathered together everyone who was involved with making day-to-day decisions for the company and created a list of every key decision we dealt with over the course of each day, week, month, and year.

From that list of about eighty items, we combined and eliminated enough of the key decisions to get us down to forty-eight items for the matrix. The key decisions ranged from approving a new hire and client refunds to selling the company and settling lawsuits.

We realized that to grow the company quickly and leverage our SOPs there would only be four tiers of approval: owner, CEO, COO, and department head.

We then went through each decision one by one and discussed who needed to be involved in the approval process. It was easy to come to a consensus on about 90 percent of the items, and it was quite a battle to agree on the remaining 10 percent.

People get kind of funny about giving up certain areas of responsibility or raising their hands for areas that they currently are not accountable for. In working with several coaching clients to create their decision matrix, this issue always comes up.

Once we had that all completed, we simply charted it out in a matrix format and implemented the matrix within our company SOP system for each department.

I want to be clear about the power of this tool in my company and the leverage it created for achieving the 40 Hour Work YEAR. When we first developed this matrix in early 2001, the owners were responsible for over twenty of the forty-eight key decisions; by the end of 2003 the owners only checked seven of the boxes!

In sharing this tool with several entrepreneurs and companies over the years, the feedback has been universal. It is simple, it works, it holds people accountable, and it keeps people in alignment with SOPs.

I have provided a sample decision matrix on the next page for you to review and to assist you in developing your own.

Decision Matrix

CORPORATE APPROVAL METHODS

Item	Approved By:	Owner	CEO	COO	DEPT HEAD
Changes in Benefit Plans			X		
Changes in 401k		X	X		
Bonus Plans		X	X	X	
Business Acquisition		X	X		
Defending Lawsuit			X		
Approve Settlements		X	X		
Approve Litigation			X		
Negotiate Contract			X	X	
Sign Contracts (Vendors)			X	X	
Review Contracts			X		
Terminate Contracts			X		
Approve Purchase Over $10k				X	
Approve Purchase Under $10k					X
Terminate Employee			X		X
Approve New Hire				X	X
Approve Promotion			X	X	
Approve Demotion				X	
Approve Merit Increase (ees except CEO/Pres)			X		
Approve Merit Increase (CEO/Pres)		X	X		
Approve Item Over Budget $				X	
Terminate Lease			X		
Sign Lease			X		
Negotiate Lease			X	X	
Review Lease Options			X	X	
Approve Bus. In New State State			X		
Approve Quotes to Prospects			X	X	
Approve Marketing Programs			X		
Approve Agent Agreements			X		
Approve Changes to Company Contract			X		
Approve Renewal Rate Increases			X	X	

More than one X per line item indicates multiple approval levels.

Decision Filter

When looking at how I could develop an accountable, focused executive team and aligned culture within my company, I knew that filtering all decisions through our values was the key. But once I started looking at company decisions on a tactical and budgetary level, the values alone were not enough.

Empowering my employees to make the key decisions necessary to grow the business, while at the same time making sure we were increasing profits, required the development of what I call a decision filter.

For our company culture and the way I view business in general, this was not difficult for me to create. The decision filter we implemented was the following:

1. Company
2. Owners
3. Employees

I messaged this to everyone in the company, and any time an employee had an issue or concern they wanted to discuss, they would first have to run it through this filter. If there was no company, if the company couldn't operate, if it couldn't meet its obligations, guess what? The owners close the business. And then, of course, there won't be a need for employees.

I'm not minimizing the importance of employees to our company, because I do believe that they are the most valuable asset. But the employees must realize where the money is coming from. If the company can't sustain paying the employees, it doesn't matter. There's no company; there's no employees.

This was a very useful filter for our company. Whenever we would look at a new purchase, venture, service, or alliance, we would run it through this filter. In my experience, the majority of entrepreneurs have this filter backwards, or worse yet, they have owners as number one.

To further define this filter, I used the questions below when making a decision:

1. Company

Will this increase the value of the company and is it in alignment with our top five priorities for the year?

2. Owners

Will this increase owner wealth without increasing business or personal risk beyond our current tolerance?

3. Employees

Do we have the staff, talent, and budget to pay our employees to execute on this decision and do they have the right mindset?

As we built our culture around this decision filter, with our core values as the lead filter, our employees knew they were working for a company that was headed in the right direction and was focused on their development and growth.

EXERCISE

How are you currently filtering the decisions you make in your company? List below three or more projects, purchases, ventures etc. that you are currently reviewing for your business

Now run each of these through the Decision Filter below and answer YES or NO to each of the three questions:

1. Company –

Will this increase the value of the company and is it in alignment with our top 5 priorities for the year?

2. Owners –

Will this increase owner wealth without increasing business or personal risk beyond our current tolerance?

3. Employees –

Do we have the staff, talent and budget to pay our employees to execute on this decision, and do they have the right mindset?

The choice is up to you.....In my experience, when we could honestly answer YES to all three, we were very successful with the projects, purchases etc. When we went against the Decision Filter by justifying away one or more of the NO answers, it was ugly....

People Plan

As we started to implement the transition plan in early 2002, 70 percent of the people who were working for the company were the "right" people, meaning they had the right mindset. However, only about 80 percent of those people were working in roles that maximized their skill set.

Upon realizing this fact, we implemented multiple types of testing for our existing employees and future hires: Behavioral testing, skill testing, culture fit, etc. By using these types of tools, we were able to match our current employee pool to the different job descriptions we had developed within our SOPs.

This saved our company tens of thousands of dollars every year. Although testing was not the panacea for our people plan, it was key to getting the right people matched up to the job duties we needed filled.

The people plan was integral to the development of our transition plan, and we used it as our reference point when adjustments in our growth forecast occurred.

We began by looking at our current organizational structure, along with the salaries, job responsibilities, and skills required for the implementation of our strategic growth plan.

We developed a six-month and one-year forecast of what our organization chart would look like as we implemented the SOPs and growth plan. After building that out, we developed an organization chart for each additional six-month period as my partner and I would remove ourselves from our duties and responsibilities.

This became rather difficult when trying to look more than a year ahead, since we had not built the company this way previously. Interestingly enough, the company was actually able to handle our duties in a more efficient manner than we had predicted in our initial people plan.

This plan was reviewed every quarter and adjusted when necessary, mainly due to exceeding our growth forecasts during the period of 2002 through 2004.

When it comes to basic people principles, I believe entrepreneurs should write down how they view their employee (people) relationships and how they want to be viewed by their employees.

Early on in my career as a manager, I relied on some basic employee rules that I still use to this day. The following rules have served me well and keep the *personal* out of the business.

Friendly, *Not* Friends: Time and time again, I hear the horror stories around this one. To create a culture of teamwork and drive toward common goals with our employees, I believe I must be friendly. To create a situation of absolute chaos within our company, I believe everyone must be friends.

In Control, *Not* Controlling: As I mentioned before, I believe that all entrepreneurs are control freaks to some degree. To realize the 40 Hour Work YEAR, I had to let go of the controlling while remaining in control. Employees know when they are being micromanaged, and although this is a great technique for getting people to quit, it is no way to build a passionate and aligned team.

Delegating, *Not* Dumping: The easiest thing we could have done during the introduction of our transition plan was to dump a bunch of to-dos and responsibilities on our team. That *would not* have worked! To delegate, we had to make sure we had the right people doing the right things and to give them the tools to be successful. Once that was taken care of (with all eight items in place), delegating was a simple task.

Firm but Fair: For me, there was no bigger compliment than when one of my employees would describe my management style as firm but fair. When an employee was asked what it was like to work for me and that was the response, I knew I had nailed the other three rules!

I buy from people, not from businesses. I invest in people, not companies. The most valuable asset we developed during the transition process was our people, especially the key managers who made up our executive team.

Developing this team was not without a few hiccups. We did replace two of the five people on our executive team during the first year. This was to be expected, and had we not made the changes, we risked losing the trust and respect of the entire company.

For operational and organizational purposes, this team consisted of a department head for each of our four departments, with the CEO as the fifth member and leader of the team. The four departments were sales, finance, HR services/payroll, and benefits.

EXERCISE

Using a separate piece of paper:

1. Draw your current Organizational Chart
2. Put a **W** by the boxes that you have weekly interaction with and an **M** by the boxes that you have monthly interaction with

Using a separate piece of paper:

1. Draw your future Organizational Chart with you performing **ZERO** job duties in the company. This means the following:
   a) Org Chart has no W's or M's (no interaction needed with you)
   b) Your current duties are covered completely
   c) You can take a 30 day vacation with NO company contact
   d) Your business operates at 80% of its current performance level or higher each month

2. Compare the two charts - Looking at your current Org Chart, which people will still be working in your company when you have ZERO job duties? List them below:

3. From the list above, place each person in the appropriate box of your future Org Chart
4. Did any of them get promoted? Demoted? Dumped?
5. For the people that were promoted on your future Org Chart, share your Vision of THEIR future in your company! For the others, I think you know what to do......

Forecasting

I am a worst-case scenario kind of guy. When developing the forecasting models for our transition plan and laying out what the following three years would look like, I started with the worst-case scenario in our sales and the worst-case scenario in our overhead.

I want to be clear about something: planning for the worst-case scenario is *not* sandbagging. I would start by meeting with my sales people to gather their individual sales goals for the year. I would take what they gave me and cut it by 30 percent. This eliminated what my partner called "sales math."

As usual, you have the 20 percent making 80 percent of the sales, but if the entire team was at $50 million for the year, I would worst-case scenario the number at $35 million. Year after year (2001 through 2006), we always hit around 20 to 25 percent under the sales team's top estimate (not the worst-case scenario).

We then took the sales forecast for the year, plugged in the seasonality factors based on historical data and market variables, and then built out our annual budgets by department. We revisited these numbers monthly and made adjustments every three months as necessary. This system was used throughout the transition plan process and every year after.

People in general like routine, and the forecasting of sales and budgets was a very stable, predictable way to align each of our departments around the overall vision and goals of the company. I am constantly amazed at the lack of process around forecasting and budgets within the companies I coach.

Conversely, I am constantly surprised by the *huge* improvements these same companies make once they implement a forecasting system throughout their entire organization.

Letting Go

When my partner and I agreed to take a pay cut and we said, "Here is the money we're spending to hire the key people and develop the systems," we also created a timeline of when each major shift in responsibility and "letting go" would occur.

This timeline was tied directly to our people plan. The owners must commit to letting go of these things by these dates. It doesn't mean we didn't shift them a little bit from time to time, but they always stayed on the list and we continued to commit to letting them go.

The whole point of the transition plan was to never have to work again, so letting go of control was always the cornerstone or our plan. To make sure we remained in alignment as owners, we had an agreement with each other. It was a simple two-sentence agreement that we updated every three months that outlined the specific areas of responsibility and related job duties that we committed to letting go. To make the 40 Hour Work YEAR a reality, we had to eventually let go of everything!

Believe me, contrary to popular entrepreneurial belief, the world will not end when you get the hell out of the way and let your people grow the company. I'm not saying it's going to be perfect. We had many stumbles and falls, but so what? We trusted our SOPs, decision matrix, decision filter, people plan, and forecasting to guide us back on track and take us to the Promised Land!

One of the main commitments we made as owners was coaching our future CEO and the executive team. As I mentioned earlier, we had to replace two of the five people that eventually made up the executive team.

Grooming the person who would eventually run the company was no easy task. On the other hand, for me, there was nothing more rewarding throughout this whole process than seeing Seth challenge himself and achieve a level of confidence beyond his wildest dreams!

The fact that I had a partner in my business made the execution of handing off our job duties to others more difficult than if I had been the sole owner. I soon discovered once the first stage of letting go was ready to occur that my partner and I were not in total alignment as to what this actually meant. It seemed like there was always a client that still needed us to be involved or a new service rollout that would require an extension of the timeline.

Of course, there were good reasons for some of these, but just realize that when a partner is involved, letting go can be more subjective at times. By sticking to our plan and trusting the process, we were eventually able to let go of everything.

Tracking Metrics

We had metrics developed in our business plan before we opened the doors, and we had basic department metrics long before we started the transition plan. As you could probably tell, I am a metric freak! What gets measured gets done. The first thing I do when starting a new venture or when coaching a new client is dig into the metrics of the company.

I believe it is vital to have no more than five key metrics that are used as a guide to the health of the business. We had five key metrics for our company, and if we hit the standards for each of those five, the company was running at 95 percent peak performance.

I meet entrepreneurs from time to time who tell me they have twenty or more metrics for their business. Once I explain that the five are for the company as a whole and should represent 95 percent of their overall performance measurements, I am usually able to help them narrow it down. Of course, we had metrics for our sales department, HR department, customer service department, etc., but those metrics all rolled up into the five key company metrics.

For me, the creation of our metrics was like making multiple recipes out of seven separate ingredients. I use the term "metric tag" when identifying each of these seven ingredients.

We began developing our metrics by creating a spreadsheet with seven columns.

1. Revenue: Revenue could be total sales, net sales, gross margin, net margin, etc. The reason we used the broad category of "revenue" was that different departments used different forms of revenue for their key metrics.

2. Expenses: Expenses include anything that you would find on the Profit & Loss Statement from labor to rent.

3. Time: We used the time column to identify daily, weekly, monthly, quarterly, and yearly metric tags. While developing our transition plan we even had some individual day parts included in this column.

4. Services/Products: This column includes all of the products and services we were offering within the company.

5. Employee: This is simply the employee count, internally or externally.

6. Department: This is a great one to use, especially when you are comparing productivity metrics across a time period between departments.

7. Region: We started expanding the business across the United States in early 2000, so state-by-state and regional comparison metrics were excellent indicators for us when it came to allocating resources and opening new markets.

I will share a few examples of how we mixed up the different tags to create simple metrics we could use to guide our company and keep pulse on our performance.

We used payroll per employee per month divided by sales per employee month. With this, we used six different ingredients to create one hell of a recipe for success: (1) expense, (2) employee, and (3) time divided by (4) revenue, (5) employee, and (6) time.

Here is another one: total sales per month divided by total sales per state per month compared to same month last year. I am a big fan of YOY (year over year), and this is a great metric for measuring everything from talent to marketing. This one also uses six metric tags: (1) revenue and (2) time, divided by (3) revenue, (4) region, and (5) time, all compared to (6) time.

As you can see, once we developed our grid with the seven different tags, we just pulled what we needed to measure to refine our business strategy and performance.

The more metric tags you incorporate in each metric, the more powerful and relevant the individual data point will be for your company. Think about the impact and relevance of a measurement such as sales per month per department compared to the same month last year instead of the basic sales per month. As the saying goes, statistics can lie, so to make metrics more reliable, increase the number of metric tags.

We spent a lot of time refining and developing our company and department key metrics. The reason they worked so well for us was that we aligned what our growth plan was with our metrics and in turn we were inspecting what we expected throughout the entire organization.

EXERCISE

What are your key ingredients for success?

Looking at your company as a whole, what are the metric tags that you use to measure performance?
List them below:

Using three to five of the above tags that you listed, create a company metric below:

Create no more than five key metrics that will allow you to measure whether your company is running at 95% of its peak performance:

1. _____

2. _____

3. _____

4. _____

5. _____

Owner Wealth & Company Value

When my partner and I agreed to reduce our compensation to build the business to a point where we didn't have to work anymore, we also wanted to make sure that the company would continue to increase our wealth.

Part of this equation was increasing the value of our equity in the company, which followed my principle of building an asset not a business. The other part of this equation was to replace the income we were putting back into the company within two years or less.

During the first six months after moving to Vegas, I would say the following quite often: "If I have to go back to work, I'm getting paid." When things would come up and one of the executive team would say, "Scott can you take care of this?" I'd say, "Fine, but the money's coming from you. We created and implemented this plan together. You're running the company. If I'm going to go back in, then I'm going to get paid."

Clarity equals power, and there are few statements I could think of that were clearer than that!

Rewarding performance is the only way to pay people in my experience. So, to ensure the company was in alignment with increasing owner wealth and company value, Seth's entire compensation structure was tied to this principle.

Because his compensation focused on maximizing these two areas, each and every decision he made for the company included this factor, as I stated earlier in the decision filter section. For example: If we buy an SQL server system and convert everything to SQL, will this increase owner wealth and value? If yes, what is the return on investment over what time period? If those measurements were acceptable and in line with our growth plan and budgets, then he would reference the decision matrix, get the appropriate sign offs, and pull the trigger.

Another example: If we open up the Dallas market, meaning we go spend a quarter million dollars and open up a Dallas office this year, over the next two years will the ROI increase owner wealth and company value? No. So, opening a Dallas office was not put in the pipe.

I learned to *leverage the filter, lose the emotion.* In my experience, entrepreneurs let emotion and ego cloud their decision making. When we trained our key employees and leaders to use the filters I have discussed in this book, we gained the power and control to make decisions that ultimately created the 40 Hour Work YEAR.

Final Thoughts

One of my favorite sayings is "plan your work, work your plan." I decided to stop chasing the shiny pennies and developed the transition plan to make sure I built a sellable asset, not a sinkable business.

Once a month I would go somewhere away from the office (not my house), turn off the crackberry, cell phone, laptop etc., and spend some time thinking about where I wanted to be in my life one year from that day. I updated my plan from month to month and constantly pushed the limits of what I thought was possible.

On the company side, once the plan was complete and implemented, we continued to update and adjust our forecasts monthly at first, then quarterly, and then finally twice a year. Making changes too frequently would not have allowed our company to flourish and we would have risked losing morale as well as trust and respect from our employees.

These were scheduled intervals, not whenever we remembered to do it. They were put in everyone's calendar, and the expectations were set at the end of each review for the next meeting.

The transition plan started with a simple goal of removing the owners from the operations equation. It ended up creating an asset that grew beyond my wildest dreams while allowing me to live the 40 Hour Work YEAR. And ultimately it made possible the sale of my company, which allowed me to coach and help grow fellow entrepreneur's businesses across America.

EXERCISE

Of the eight key transition plan areas, which have I implemented?

Which of the eight still need work?

For each of the eight key transition plan areas, how would I rank my company regarding implementation on a scale of 1 to 10, with 10 being perfect?

    ____Standard Operating Procedures
    ____Decision Matrix
    ____Decision Filter
    ____People Plan
    ____Forecasting
    ____Letting Go
    ____Tracking Metrics
    ____Owner Wealth & Company Value

EXERCISE *(continued)*

How would I rank each key member of my management team?

Do I have a team that could start creating my transition plan?

What do I want my role to be in my company one year from today?

What does that look like?

EXERCISE *(continued)*

Now create three action steps that you will take in the next ninety days to begin moving your life to where you want it to be ... who knows, you may want to live the 40 Hour Work YEAR.

Based on this Chapter:

What did I learn about my business?

What did I learn about myself?

10

Enjoy Life,
Make Money,
Do Deals

It was January 2004. I had been living in Vegas for about a year and a half, my partner and I were totally removed from working in or on the business, and Human Capital had just been named to the Inc. 500 list for the first time. I was truly enjoying life!

During this period is of time, we were operating as what I call an enterprise business. We had developed and implemented scalable systems. There was a five-person executive team accountable for *every* aspect of the business, and we were now operating in thirty states across the United States.

Moving to Vegas had opened my eyes to the reality that we needed to expand outside of the Midwest region to help diversify our risk and capture higher margins. During late 2002, we opened up our first POD (point of distribution) in a couple of states.

Each POD was an independent branch of our company with its own investors and SOPs for sales and marketing. The Michigan HQ was the back office for all of the clients brought on by the individual POD, but we did not have to bear the cost of opening and staffing these sales branches or any of the marketing expenses incurred.

By 2004 we had opened PODs in Nevada, Washington, Oregon, Montana, and an industry focused niche POD in Michigan.

The POD system allowed us to attain several of the goals I had in mind while developing my program: (1) reach $100 million in annual revenue, (2) open at least five sales offices across the United States, and (3) reduce Midwest region revenue to 50 percent of total company sales.

There is no way we would have reached these goals this quickly without the POD system, and there is no way we could have executed the POD system without the transition plan.

At this time, my focus filter was definitely ordered as enjoy life, make money, do deals. I was working one and a half hours a month (eighteen hours a year), inspecting what I expected. This meant reviewing the key metrics that made this engine run, reviewing the P&L, and calculating how big my distribution would be from the twenty-plus companies that made up our organization.

To pull off this quick monthly phone call with the CEO, COO, myself, and my partner required a very structured agenda and meeting rhythm that did not deviate from month to month.

We received via e-mail all of the financial documents one week before the scheduled call, which was always the last Tuesday of every month. So we could review twenty-three companies in as short a time period as possible, we developed a system in which the accounting department would match up the monthly numbers with our growth plan and metrics.

They would look for any numbers that were outliers to the plan and would place a red triangle in that specific cell of the Excel spreadsheet that would give an explanation when reviewed.

Accompanying all of the documents was a one-page summary from the controller referencing the specific areas of interest (red triangles) for our review.

The owners and the CEO had one week to contact the accounting department with any questions or clarifications regarding the summary and numbers. Silence is acceptance in my view, and we did not waste time asking questions on the call about items that were already explained.

We spent the hour and a half discussing the productive action steps the company would be taking to improve the numbers and who would be following up on the plan adjustments.

That accounts for eighteen of the forty hours. I spent the final twenty two hours a year with the executive team in Michigan or in Las Vegas. This included a two-day (sixteen-hour) strategic retreat where my role was to continue driving and focusing the vision of the company. Additionally, we held a short day (six hours) priority update session where we focused on taking the pulse of the company at midyear.

If you do the math, what do you have? The 40 Hour Work YEAR!

Because I had totally transformed myself from working in and on the business to being a passive investor and advisor, it truly was just like one of my Angel investments. The difference was that it paid me a lot more on a consistent basis.

Based on this Chapter:

What did I learn about my business?

What did I learn about myself?

11

The Position

I was now living the life I had set out to create, and the company was exceeding every goal I could imagine. My ownership paradox was shooting off the axis (in the right direction) and I had time to spend with my family, to travel, to coach other entrepreneurs, and to chase Angel deals.

It was May 2006 and we had just completed our midyear pulse check with the executive team. My partner and I met with our CPA before I headed to the airport to catch my plane back to Vegas. We had been discussing tax planning and the state of our industry in general when the topic of selling the company came up.

I don't remember exactly how it came up or who brought it up, but there it was. My partner and I had discussed selling or doing a recapitalization of the company a couple times, but this was different. Our CPA said that he was seeing strong valuations and multiples in our industry again and thought we should give it some thought. We discussed options for about a half hour and agreed to talk again the following week.

So in June of 2006, we discussed the pros and cons of selling and agreed with the help of our CPA to begin the process of selling the company.

I have this discussion with *a lot* of entrepreneurs. I am of the opinion that whether we wanted to sell or not, we should position our company as though it could be sold at any time for the right price. Because when we positioned our company for sale, we automatically increased the value of the entire asset beyond the value of our client list, equipment, building, systems, or people.

When I say position our company for sale, I am talking about the following points:

1. Having a CEO overseeing the entire company
2. Holding the executive team accountable for every aspect of performance
3. Holding a strategy meeting *every* year with midyear pulse check

4. Setting the top five priorities for the company over one-, two-, and three-year periods

5. Ensuring owners are passive investors and visionary in their leadership

6. Reducing YOY costs while increasing sales

7. Having systems-dependent operations

8. Maintaining a spotless reputation within the industry

9. *NO* company debt

10. Being at or above *all* industry standards in *all* margin areas

11. YOY client retention in the top 10 percent of the industry

12. YOY growth in the top 10 percent of industry

13. Being a nationwide player

14. Having *no* outstanding litigation

15. Having *no* single client making up over 5 percent of total sales or margin

So how did I accomplish all of these points?

1. *Having a CEO overseeing the entire company.* As I outlined earlier, this was already in place and was a huge factor in positioning our company for sale. Any prospective buyer knew that they could take over the company and not have to worry about finding a CEO, or worse yet, having to take the spot themselves.

2. *Holding the executive team accountable for every aspect of performance.* All team members' compensation and review criteria were tied to the performance of the company. While positioning our company for sale, we obviously wanted to make sure everything looked as good as possible and was running like a well-oiled machine. With the executive team being completely accountable in each of their respective departments, there was

no need for putting out fires or dealing with the urgent outweighing the important.

3. *Holding a strategy meeting every year with midyear pulse check.* We had an annual strategy meeting each of the ten years we owned the company. From the first year with three employees to the last year with close to fifty. Positioning your company requires constant and consistent planning. Making sure your company is firing on all cylinders at maximum potential means checking all of the metrics against your plans twice per year away from the office with no distractions and complete strategic focus. These events should also be facilitated by someone not involved with the company so that the owners and executive team can fully participate in the strategic plan for the following year.

4. *Setting the top five priorities for the company over one-, two-, and three-year periods.* This exercise occurred at our annual strategy retreat and was absolutely key to positioning our company within the top tier of our industry. Having your company goals and objectives is a good start, but when we were able to set up a top five prioritized list with action steps for each priority, we had complete alignment within our company.

5. *Ensuring owners are passive investors and visionary in their leadership.* My partner and I had totally removed ourselves from the operations of the company and were truly passive investors in our own business. Our role was to act as visionaries for what the future looked like for our company and to help our key leaders see the same vision we did. From the transition to the position, the vision for what everyone was working toward was the starting point for each of our strategic decisions.

6. *Reducing YOY costs while increasing sales.* As we started to discuss some of the areas we wanted to tighten up in the company to

make it the most appealing as possible, the topic of cost reduction was at the top of the list. We had always shown YOY increases in sales, but some of the expense line items had been drifting upward over the past two years. By tweaking a couple of our strategic priorities and implementing some outsourced solutions, we were able to show decreasing costs in both 2006 and 2007 while continuing to increase sales.

7. Having *systems-dependent operations.* As I discussed in detail during the SOP section, my company was built to be system-dependent, *not* owner-dependent. Positioning our company for a potential sale made this all the more crucial as we found out later. The company that ended up purchasing our business had done several previous acquisitions and the owner was very hands-off. The combination of a systems-dependent company and a CEO in place who was not the owner, made us too good to true.

8. *Maintaining a spotless reputation within the industry.* When I coach my clients on sales topics, I often reference the fact that our competitors sent us clients and prospects on more than one occasion. These were not the bottom-feeder-type clients, these were clients that for complexity or multistate reasons could not be serviced by the PEO they were currently using or quoting. I can think of no other example of a spotless reputation than having your competitors send you high-quality clients. Like the saying goes, something you pay *a lot* of money for but you can never buy—your *reputation.*

9. NO *company debt.* When it came to positioning our company and comparing our business model with others in our space, this one was a big deal. In my experience, having *no* debt in most businesses is unheard of. Both my partner and I had a strong stance on this one, and as I mentioned before, once we

paid off the small SBA loan, we never went back. I am not saying that we would have been in a bad position if we had debt, but it sure made for a stronger balance sheet and cash flow statement.

10.   *Being at or above* all *industry standards in* all *margin areas.* This point was a goal of ours from the day we turned on the lights and hung our shingle. By the time we implemented the transition plan, we had achieved this goal, and we steadily improved on this area throughout the remaining years that we owned the business. Of course there were some off months and even a couple quarters, but YOY and against the PEO industry as a whole, we were at or above the annual published margins.

11.   *YOY client retention in the top 10 percent of the industry.* I am asked quite often how I measured sales performance within the non-sales departments of our company, and my reply is always the same: *retention.* From day one, I told all of my employees that they were sales people but they just didn't know it yet. Are you familiar with the phrase "it is easier to keep a client than to find a new one"? I agree with this statement with just one caveat: I would put the word "good" in front of "client." The beauty of aligning our company with this positioning point is that once we had removed all of the bottom feeders, it was much easier to retain the clients. These clients were with us for the services and benefits we actually provided, not for some discount price or weekly special. Our operation's employees were reviewed, rewarded, and reprimanded based on the client-retention metric. Inspect what you expect.

12.   *YOY growth in the top 10 percent of the industry.* As I mentioned earlier, we made the 2003 Inc. 500 list (ranked number 151) and one of our POD companies made the list in 2004. Both times we made the list by achieving five-year growth

percentages in excess of 1,000 percent. No doubt about it, that landed us in the top 10 percent of the industry.

I think a big part of the reason we were able to grow at such a rate for a prolonged period of time was due to a specific mindset I followed and instilled in my sales people. Close the client and get the hell out of the way. I trained all my sales people to look at acquiring a client like dating. There's the meeting, first date, second date, third date, engagement, and marriage. For our company, the engagement was the contract and the marriage was the employee enrollment. Once the enrollment was done, the client was married to Human Capital, *not* the sales person. There were clients I took all the way through marriage back in 1998 that were still with the company in 2007 who I never personally communicated with for ten years. The key was that they were married to the company instead of the sales person. Obviously when positioning our company, sales growth was not only a big part of looking good for potential buyers, it was part of our "grow or die" philosophy.

13. *Being a nationwide player.* By 2007 we had clients with worksite employees in over forty states. The company that ended up buying us had operations in seventeen states, so the additional access and presence was a key positioning point for them. I mentioned earlier that I knew we needed to diversify our geographical footprint for risk and margin reasons. However, this nationwide status also gave us a unique competitive advantage against most of our competition. Very few PEOs can handle clients with multistate operations due to the complexity of employment laws and the diversity of state-run benefit plans. The ability of our clients to place employees in

most any state with just a phone call was an excellent retention and closing tool.

14. *Having* no *outstanding litigation.* Lawsuits are just part of the game in the employment administration space. Operating nationwide and posting sales of $100 million plus didn't help either. Our view of litigation was usually one of minimize, monetize, and mediate. Our CEO was an attorney, and from a positioning standpoint, keeping the lawsuits to a minimum was always in his top five priorities. If we were facing legal action, we started by putting dollars to it and weighing the settlement costs against potential legal costs. And finally, whenever possible, we would opt for mediation as a first option. Knowing that this was our view of litigation and cleaning up a couple outstanding issues was a valuable positioning point for our potential buyers.

15. *Having* no *single client making up over 5 percent of the total sales or margin.* I saved the best for last. To position your company for a long-lasting run, this point is critical. After we got burned in our second year of business, I vowed to never have more than 10 percent of my sales with any one client. As our company grew, I moved the percentage down to 5 percent. Had we not sold the business, we would have continued to lower the percentage target. In the letters of interest we got from several potential buyers, this was an item they all wanted confirmation of. The fact that we only had one client that made up 4.8 percent of our total sales and the next largest was under 2 percent was a big factor in getting the deal done and the final valuation.

Added benefits abound when your company runs in position mode. Your employees and management team raise the bar on their standards, and expectations from new hires are set at the beginning. Company meetings become laser-focused on the good, margin-producing clients versus the client that yells the loudest. Tweaking systems and SOPs are the first step when resolving client or vendor issues instead of blaming and finger pointing.

As I said before, putting yourself in this mindset is essential, whether you are going to sell your company or not. Once you have completed the transition and put your company in the right position, an acquisition for you or someone else is quick and painless.

EXERCISE

Use these following questions and tips to refine each of the fifteen points from the previous pages:

1. Having a CEO overseeing entire company
   Do you have this person currently in your company? (Not YOU)

2. Holding the executive team accountable for every aspect of performance
   How many of these team members do you currently have?

3. Holding a strategy meeting EVERY year with mid-year pulse
   Are both of these meetings scheduled? If no, schedule them NOW

4. Setting the top 5 priorities for the company over one, two and three years
   Are these completed and up to date?

5. Ensuring owners are passive investors and visionary in their leadership
   Are you? If no, do you have a plan?

6. Reducing YOY costs while increasing sales
   Is this messaged to your entire company? Are you rewarding your top performers?

7. Having systems dependent operations
   Are your systems so good that you don't even know you have them?

8. Maintaining a spotless reputation within the industry
   Are you being referred business by your competitors?

9. NO Company Debt
   How does your balance sheet look? Do you have a debt reduction plan?

10. Being at or above ALL industry standards in ALL margin areas
    Do you message this to your entire company? Are you rewarding your top performers?

11. YOY client retention in TOP 10% of industry
    Do you message this to your entire company? Are you rewarding your top performers?

12. YOY growth in TOP 10% of industry
    Do you message this to your entire company? Are you rewarding your top performers?

13. Being a nationwide player
    Have you created an expansion plan? Can someone in your company execute this plan?

14. Having no outstanding litigation
    Do you have strong legal counsel internally or externally in multiple disciplines? Have you set company limits?

15. Having no single client making up over 5% of total sales or margin
    Are you targeting squirrels, buffalo and elephants? Can your sales team hunt all three?

EXERCISE

Below is an exercise that will help with the positioning of your company. Please answer the questions, and if you have partners, have them complete this as well.

Would you buy your company today?

If yes, what would you pay?

Do you love what you currently do?

Whether you answered YES or NO, define why.

Are you running your business, or is it running you?

If it is running you, what three steps will you take in the next thirty days to change that?

Based on this Chapter:

What did I learn about my business?

What did I learn about myself?

12

Continued Success

As I reflect on my journey as an entrepreneur up to this point, I realize that each milestone was precipitated by a shift in my mindset. Once I embraced the fact that by shifting my mindset, I was able to create positive changes for everyone in my life, the strategic and tactical challenges that had once seemed so daunting were now just part of the plan.

I believe that everyone can shift their mindset in the direction that best suits what they enjoy doing in life. Once an entrepreneur realizes that this change is constant, each new shift becomes more natural and confidence inspiring.

As my story illustrates, when I combined the ingredients of passion, focus, and team with this entrepreneurial mindset, the final product was naturally

The 40 Hour Work YEAR!

To learn more, visit:

40hourworkyear.com

Thoughts, Ideas & Actions

Thoughts, Ideas & Actions

Thoughts, Ideas & Actions

Thoughts, Ideas & Actions